BUTTON

by Carole Patullo
and Jane Bayly

CURRENCY PRESS

⊕ LA MAMA

CURRENCY PLAYS

First published in 2013
by Currency Press Pty Ltd,
PO Box 2287, Strawberry Hills, NSW, 2012, Australia
enquiries@currency.com.au
www.currency.com.au

in association with La Mama Theatre, Melbourne

NATIONAL LIBRARY OF AUSTRALIA CIP DATA
Author: Patullo, Carole, author.
Title: Button / Carole Patullo, Jane Bayly and Melanie Beddie.
ISBN: 9780868199856 (paperback)
Series: Current theatre series.
Subjects: Australian drama—21st century.
Other Authors/Contributors:
                     Bayly, Jane, author.
                     Beddie, Melanie, author.
Dewey Number: A822.4
Typeset by Claire Grady for Currency Press.
Cover design by Robin Griffiths—DazzleCreative, from a concept by Carole Patullo.
Cover photograph by Thomas Lim and Zac Couyant.

Currency Press acknowledges the Traditional Owners of the Country on which we
live and work. We pay our respects to all Aboriginal and Torres Strait Islander
Elders, past and present.

Contents

Button was first performed for La Mama's Explorations Season at La Mama, Carlton, on 4 November 2011, with the following cast:

WOMAN A	Carole Patullo
WOMAN B	Jane Bayly
MUSICIAN	Peter Farnan

Consultant Director / Dramaturg, Melanie Beddie
Musician / Sound Designer, Peter Farnan
Designer, Dayna Morrissey
Lighting Designer / Operator, Katie Sfetkidis

Carole, Jane and Melanie continued developing the text and in 2012 *Button* received venue and technical assistance from Melbourne Theatre Company's Open Door Lawler residencies program. Choreographer Luke George and Designer Melanie Liertz joined the creative team and the resulting draft was performed at Frankston and Southern Peninsula Arts Centres. This printed edition of *Button* was first produced at La Mama Courthouse. Please see the program at the end of the playtext for the full details.

ACKNOWLEDGEMENTS

For development support, we would like to thank: La Mama's Explorations Season, 2011: Liz Jones, Maureen Hartley, Nedd Jones, Bec Etchell, Bryn Cullen and staff.

Melbourne Theatre Company's Open Door Lawler residencies program for venue and technical assistance, 2012: Aidan Fennessy, Mark Wheeler, Josh Noble, Frank Stoffels, Martina Murray and staff.

Frankston Arts Centre's Cube 37 for venue assistance, 2012: Merryn Tinkler, Adam Cartwright, Darren McKenzie and staff.

VCA School of Theatre for rehearsal space.

Thanks also to: Audiences from each development season for their valuable feedback and all others who have supported the project; Yoni Prior, Chris Thompson, Maude Davey, Suzanne Chaundy, Nathan King, Michael Johnson, Ariel Johnson, Tarn Johnson, Maudie Farnan, Stella Farnan; Sîan Jenkins, Paul O'Beirne and the team at Currency Press, Alex Adsett, Geoff Paine and Ready to Roll.

SONGS

'In the Seams' by Jane Bayly, Peter Farnan and Carole Patullo.
'Am I Here' by Peter Farnan. (This song first appeared in *Infectiou$* by Maude Davey and Marcia Ferguson, 1993.)
'Birds', 'Things I Haven't Done Yet', 'Not Dead Yet' and 'In Between' by Jane Bayly.

DIRECTOR'S NOTE

The process of making *Button* has been a gradual one. It has taken 18 months of working on the floor, intense discussion and then reworking to generate the text we publish here. It remains a work in progress. New elements continue to emerge and some things get discarded or remade. These choices are informed by our experience of showing it to audiences and discovering how the theatricality of the piece works in performance.

The play grew out of a desire by Jane and Carole to create a show for themselves from scratch. As actors they frequently work on newly made performances and with new writing. This project gives them the opportunity to flex their own writing muscles and to enjoy the artistic autonomy of being the initiating artists.

Button is a piece about how friendship can be a difficult and delicate negotiation and how, as it matures, it has many shifts and phases. It is a piece that celebrates life whilst recognising our interconnectedness to the natural cycles of change and decay. At its core *Button* is about how individuals are woven together into a community by the many threads of the natural world, social conventions and human needs.

The performance's creation has been truly collaborative. It exists both on the page and in the collective minds and bodies of me, Carole and Jane. The text began as a series of individual pieces which emerged from writing workshops and together we have developed it into a blueprint for a theatrical performance. It works on both a conscious narrative level and as a metaphoric and poetic text. The spoken language is delicate and at times lyrical and yet is only one layer of this work. Of equal importance are the physical languages of gesture, dance and illusion. Alongside this exist the songs and music which lift the piece away from a direct narrative and into a world of its own.

The piece is multi-layered and textured, unpretentious and much loved by all of us who made it. It is like a quilt which brings together many elements, thoughts and styles and creates from them a whole from which many patterns can be discerned. In many ways the strength of *Button* is its personal and handcrafted quality. The piece comes from our hearts.

Button has had many wonderful artists contributing to its creation, each bringing their expertise and passion to the work. What has inspired all of us is the honesty and humour of the initial concept by Jane and Carole.

I hope you enjoy *Button* as much as we enjoyed making it.

WRITERS' NOTE

Button is the product of a joyful collaborative process. We wish to acknowledge Jenny Kemp and her Generative Writing workshops for inspiring and propelling us to find our writer's voices. Melanie's dramaturgical input has been invaluable from the outset, and we thank her for her astute questions, guidance and encouragement at every step. Each collaborating artist has enriched the theatricality of the piece and we thank them all for their skills and generosity.

Carole Patullo and Jane Bayly

FOR STUDENTS

Button uses various theatrical conventions to weave together the stories and dreams of Woman A and Woman B. The non-linear narrative reveals story and character through dance, gesture, direct address, conversational dialogue, internal poetic monologue, song, theatrical illusion, silence and stillness. The musician creates live sound onstage, looping sounds and playing instruments to accompany the original songs. The choreography explores various qualities and abstractions of everyday actions, using rhythm, repetition, motif and spatial patterns and tensions. Transformations of time and place are signified by the actors' gestures, physicality and spatial relationships between the actors, design elements and the audience. Lighting enhances these aspects and, together with the design, encourages the audience to imagine or 'fill in' the surroundings / negative space and to consider the representational significance of objects and set elements.

CHARACTERS

A, a middle-aged woman who lives alone. Somewhat childlike, she wears clothing not quite from the present time. This clothing must have buttons.

B, a middle-aged woman who lives alone. Somewhat reserved, she wears comfortable clothing appropriate for walking. This clothing must include a polar fleece item.

SETTING

There are two chairs—one lived in and worn (A's place), the other clean and new (B's place).

A spider web emanates skywards behind the worn chair.

Autumnal leaf litter is scattered near the new chair.

Beyond is blackness.

The musician, with instruments and equipment, is clearly visible onstage and occasionally interacts with the action.

Space and time are fluid.

In Hyperspace, the women are alone, suspended in time and place but strangely connected through thought.

SONGS / SOUND DESIGN

The musician creates a live sound score and accompanies the original songs.

PHYSICAL SEQUENCES AND CHOREOGRAPHY

The piece contains a number of short gestural dances built from everyday movements, in which A and B sometimes move in unison and sometimes in counterpoint. Choreographed movement accompanies the songs.

A and B enter. A is holding a tin of shortbread. B is holding a cushion. They stand by their chairs and momentarily face the audience. They sit, A in her chair, and B on the arm of hers.

The sound of time.

Unaware of each other, they sing: 'In the Seams'.

A: Fresh cotton sheets

           Being in the library

           Cream cheese icing… ooh

B: Smooth cotton sheets

           Running down a sand dune

           Chicken soup… ooh

BOTH: Ooh ooh ooh

           Ooh ooh oooooooooooh

A: Big blackbird

           Singing at my window

           Hello!... Gone

B: My loved one

           Singing in the kitchen… gone

A: Am I the only one

B: Am I the only one

A: Am I the only one

B: Am I the only one

A: Am I the only one

B: Am I the only one
A: Am I the only one
B: Am I the only one

BOTH: Somewhere in between
        Living in the seams
        Somewhere in between
        Living in the seams

B: Close my eyes
        The great big sky… ooh
A: Plunge my hands
        In a can of worms… ooh

A: Am I the only one
B: Am I the only one
A: Am I the only one
B: Am I the only one

BOTH: Somewhere in between
        Living in the seams
        Somewhere in between
        Living in the seams
        In between
        In my dreams
        In between
        In the seams

Physical sequence one: Each woman finds herself alone, shudders and then inspects the world around her.

A *speaks to the audience.*

A: Not long after she moved in, I'd hear a noise and imagine what she was doing: ironing a new dress to go to the theatre; dinner with the Spanish man who taught her flamenco; preparations for her research work at the Howard Florey Institute; dragging the body of the pizza delivery guy who was inexcusably late. Rubbing her body down with hydrating moisturiser after a loofing; eating Chicken Tonight and doing Sudoku; reading that Dan Brown or Virginia Woolf. Sitting in an office chair with a fox fur and gumboots on, a mirror positioned down below.

> *She turns to* B.

When I get to know you, all the infinite possibility will be gone.

> A *approaches* B*'s space.* A *has shortbread heart biscuits in a tin—a welcome gift for the new neighbour.* A *knocks.*

Hello!

> B *hides.*

Hello-o!

Are you there?

Are you there?

> A *looks at the biscuits. She eats one and returns to her place.*

Physical sequence two: Each woman sits in her chair. Time passes. The real world intrudes; fantasies and fears erupt.

Each in her chair. A *stares at her button jar;* B *holds her cushion.*

B: I didn't want to bring our pillows to my new place. So I did some research. The right pillow can help you face each day rejuvenated and fresh. You spend a third of your time with your pillow; it's one of the most intimate relationships you'll have. You need to choose carefully from the infinite set of possibilities. I was offered twelve shape and density profiles with various synthetic or natural fills. I chose feather. I was warned about dust mites—they live off our dead skin. I don't mind; it's a comfort to provide nourishment, share a meal. I miss that.

A feather drops. She shudders.

Things to do. Life to live.

B *has been out walking.* A *intercepts her on the path outside.*

A: [*holding out a jar of buttons*] I'm hoping you might be able to open this for me? I've tried, tried everything. I've seen you head off on your walks… you look kind of fit and strong, so I thought you'd be a good person to ask.

B: Okay…

A: I've always had old buttons. I got two jars from my Nan and even when I was little, I remember I used to like tipping them out on the bed to sort through. It was exciting, because there were always a few gems; little hand painted or embossed amongst the pedestrian, everyday ones. I still have some of those special ones; I can't bring myself to use them. See look at that one.

B: I can't really say I've ever had much interest in them.

A: But you like this one don't you? Look at that detail. You just don't see buttons like that now, or at least I don't. A treasure. I like to imagine what they could have been used for: pieces for a board game, betting chips for cards, money for playing shops. Or what was it on? Eyes on a teddy, a mohair cardigan? Why did it come off? Ripped? Was it child's clothing or adult? Female? Yes, I think definitely female.

B: Yes, probably. I tend to wear polar fleece.

A: I cannot imagine this button on a polar fleece.

B: Why keep them if you don't like to use them?

A: Well I like them and they will come in handy some day.

I use the ordinary ones. That's what I'm doing now, searching for one for my pyjamas.

A *proffers the jar to* B.

B: I'd just get a new pair.

A: Really?

B *averts her eyes and takes the jar.*

B: Ooh this is on tight!

A: But all they need is a button. The pyjamas are just fine; a bit worn but that has made them soft and familiar.

B *opens the jar and hands it back.*

Well done! I knew you'd get it. I wouldn't ever get rid of something because it needed a button. That seems very reckless. I even get worried about socks.

B: Socks?

A: No-one darns now. It's such a shame. I don't want to forget... not so long ago people took care to darn socks.

B: Life's too short.

A: How come, you busy working at the How... socialising?

B: Working, living, like everyone.

A: Yes. Well if you sewed on a button here and there, you mightn't need to work so hard!

B: Oh come on—

A: Well in a way, it's symbolic. That button, of an attitude.

B: What attitude? Not wanting to fill my life with clutter!

A: Sorry you seem cross, I've irritated you.

B: No I'm not... it's just... you can go to Target and get socks and PJs for virtually nothing.

A: Someone's still made them though, even if they've been paid a pittance to do it.

B: Yes, I suppose so...

A: Yes, well thanks for opening the jar.

B: No problem.

A: Now we've met we should have a cup of tea or something sometime.

B: Yes.

A: Well I know where you live. Hah!

> B *flees back to her place.* A *returns to hers, disappointed.*

B: Breathe. Breathe.

The ecstatic roar of the Great Big Nothing.

> *She fills her lungs; looks up.*

The open sky!

Breathe.

The sky and me. Beyond it all.

> *She shuts her eyes and imagines being free.*

> *She is a bird: wings wide, she crows with pleasure and soars high on her chair top.*

> *She loops and slams headfirst into a wall, out cold.*

A: Shoosh!

Button it, button up, zip it. Sshh… shut it, shut up.

> A*'s attention is captured by something.*

What is that?

Bruised wood, broom vigilance.

Crust, carrot end, a bead all lurking in the shadows.

Grease, spills, dirt, hair, nail holes, a button, pin, thread…

B: [*picking herself up from the floor*] Smashed against the rocks, brittle bones, anaemia, dystopia, blind to opportunities, un-neighbourly attitude, inconsistent, act your age, get over it…

> *They crawl towards the future in unison.*

A: [*together*] Big things, little things… an ingrown hair, the famine, feathers, stardust, a noise through the wall…

B: [*together*] Big things, little things… an open map, dinner on the table, feathers, stardust, a noise through the wall…

A: Remains of the day…

B: No evidence of a cohesive plan…

A: A stitch in time…

B: Mountains to climb…

A: A stain, a stain, a stain that leads me to it.

Think familiar blood, bloody blood, dried and crusty on the carpet edge.

Closer, looking, not food, no not food… dare to touch it?

Black spider cuddles a cockroach, crunching the shell in its mandibles.

Another watches on, already embalmed.

This is all happening every moment, every day before our very eyes conjured. We cannot escape this, this demise, this drive upon us to complete the cycle:

Birth—

BOTH: Life, death.

Physical sequence three: Each woman shudders and then inspects the world before her.

A spider makes its presence felt.

Hyperspace:

A: I can hear you—life.

B: Life outside my door.

A: In the trees, on the floor.

B: Buzzing, clicking, calling.

A: Making your presence felt.

B: I know you are there.

A: I'm not invisible, I do exist.

B: I do exist. I'm still here.

A: I didn't imagine being here. Like this.

B: Funny where you end up.

A: Is this the end?

B: There's a thought.

> *They are at their letterboxes. From nowhere, mail appears in their hands:* A *has a junk mail catalogue;* B *holds a handwritten envelope.*

A: Ooh—a card! Lucky you!

B: I'd have thought you'd have one of those no junk mail stickers.

A: I hate an empty letterbox.

> *Both return to their chairs.*

> *Physical sequence four:* A *lies on the floor.* B *lies back in her chair, as if in the bath. Each looks at her mail.*

> *After a while, each discards it.*

> *Through the window,* A *notices a bird.*

> *As* A *speaks,* B *resumes her physical sequence, reminiscing in the bath.* B *simultaneously speaks the words in italics.*

A: Little birdy in the cherry blossom. How light he must be in that tree. Holding on to flimsy branches, birdy boy is *hoping* I'll come out. He's *waiting* for me. His *mouth* is open, *ready*, that birdy boy wants to *kiss*. Kiss me.

> *She puckers and kisses.*

Ooh, ooh.

Make sure you *don't struggle* like a little wormy caught in his beak.

You'll have to do it.

Birdy boy might want *more*—to touch your hair, your bottomo. *Pull you close.*

Ruffle your feathers and not *let you go.*

He might snatch you away to his sticky place.

Oh birdy boy will enjoy that.

I'll nest with birdy boy.

Payment—a touch of my dark mystery.

His beak might be sharp.

Better watch out—he might tear me apart.

But the fruit is juicy here.

Willing, you come into my lair.

The promise of plump worms your beak prepares.

Each notices birds in the sky. Separately, they sing their thoughts: 'Birds'.

BOTH: Birds watch us making patterns on the ground

They see us scramble here and there

Hanging out washed underwear

Birds can rise

Glide above it all

Looking on as the big things grow small

They see what we carry in

What we toss away

What we plant

What we dig up

How long we choose to stay

They know whose doors are open

Know who has a key

Who's got what in whose back shed

Who you are and what you did

Whose neighbours are left for dead…

They face each other for a moment.

Without acknowledging each other, they simultaneously move as they sing:

Birds learn how to fly before they fall

Overcoming gravity

Doing what comes naturally

Birds can choose to leave the earth behind

Navigating by the sun

Not weighed down by anyone

Feathers fall.

Hyperspace:

B: Things get in.

A: Things happen.

B: Life force. In our hair.

A: On our tongues.

B: Munching on our skin.

A: We're all hosts.

B: We're all parasites.

A: All the same.

BOTH: Billions of organisms. Inhabiting.

B: Inside everything.

A: Under everything.

B: Behind everything.

BOTH: Unstoppable.

A: Birth, life…

BOTH: Death.

A: Things break down.

B: Things come apart.

I've been told I need a surgeon. I need a surgeon with steady hands that don't slip. I hope his instruments are bright and sharp. I don't want to be rough cut. I need to be repaired.

A: No-one darns now.

They look at each other momentarily.

B: No.

A: I imagined being here.

B: Funny where you end up.

A: Here we are.

B: Just bodies with heads. Sucking in oxygen.

A: Making a mess.

B: A chip, a crack, a broken wing.

A: Thread the needle and fix the thing.

B: Scar on the knee.

A: Hole in the heart.

B: All I need is a replacement part.

A: Undo my buttons.

B: Give me some air.

A: Open me up.

BOTH: See what's there.

They look at each other.

B *is on a walking track.* A *follows her.*

A: Why do you walk?

B: It makes me feel good. The body electric!

A: Keep young? You do look young.

B: That's part of it I suppose. 'Use it, or lose it.'

> B *keeps the pace up. Undeterred,* A *makes conversation.*

A: I've been wondering where birds go to die.

> B *stops in her tracks.*

You never see their little skeletons anywhere.

B: No… they must be in the leaf litter.

> B *walks.* A *checks the leaf litter, then catches up with* B.

A: I don't remember any jokes anymore… except a puerile one I learnt when I was about seven.

> B *stops.*

B: What is it?

A: No, it's really stupid, a dumb play on words.

B: Go on, tell it.

A: Mmmn. Well a lady loses her dog called Titswobble, so she goes to the police and says to the policeman 'Have you seen my tits wobble?' He says 'No, but I'd like to'.

B: That's pretty bad.

A: It really disturbs me that it's the only one I remember.

B: I've never been that good with jokes… I only know a couple.

A: Goodo!

B: What's the one thing you can hold but can't touch? A conversation.

A: Oh wait, you didn't give me time to guess.

B: I don't know joke etiquette. It's more of a riddle anyway.

A: Yes, and the other one.

B: What is the sharpest thing in the world?

> A fart; it goes through your pants and doesn't even leave a hole.

A: That's as childish as mine, but it is funny.

B: Age is a very high price to pay for maturity.

A: Too true.

They arrive at a view, high up looking out, and take in the panorama.

A sea of little tiled rooftops… cheek by jowl.

B: That's Stillwaters.

A: I know. I shudder when I see the ads.

B: Yes.

A: 'Over fifty-five? Your new life awaits!'

B: Not far away…

A: Mmmn I can't imagine being there.

Trapped. Stagnant Waters. Atrophying in a unit on Retirement Avenue. Activity night with bingo Bev. Determined to win—

BOTH: The meat tray.

A: Manicured lawns.

B: Coloured wood-chips.

A: 'Small dogs only'.

B: Twenty-four hour surveillance.

A: Hawaiian themed nights.

B: An onsite hairdresser.

A: Podiatry on call.

B: Well that might be okay, I've got a few corns—from bush walking.

A: See, next you'll be in a zipped velour tracksuit and a pair of cumfs.

It's a shame. I don't feel any different—inside I'm still twenty-five.

B: Yes, betrayed… I finally get my head together and my body starts falling apart.

A: No-one really sees us now.

B: I didn't imagine there'd be a use-by date.

A: I was thinking about those cougar ladies—you know—that go after younger men. I think it's the same for them. They just can't accept the physical decline.

B: No, that's something else… leopard print and fake tan.

A: Mmmn, well they certainly make sure they're not invisible. I wonder what animal print I would be?

They sing together, in conversation: 'Things I Haven't Done Yet.'

B: What do I regret?

         The first cigarette

         And the next

A: And the next

B: And the next

         What do I regret?

         Bouncing that cheque

A: Not getting on that jet

         Guilty

B: I object

BOTH: There are things I haven't done yet

         Things I haven't done yet

         Things we haven't done yet

         What do I expect?

         When I stand in the rain

B: I'll get wet

A: I'll get wet

BOTH: I'll get wet

         What will happen next?

         Place your bets

         I might collect or spiral into debt

         They dance, tentative but playful.

         So many things I haven't done yet

Things I haven't done yet

Things I haven't done yet

They move their chairs closer together.

So many things I haven't done yet

Things I haven't done yet

Things I haven't done yet

All the things I haven't done yet

Haven't even begun yet

Are we having fun yet?

They are at B*'s place.* A *sits in* B*'s chair.*

A: A while back, I went outside through the laundry door to check if the washing was dry. As it banged shut, I saw something move above me; it was a black house spider, hanging upside down under the beam. I thought it was very odd.

B: Why?

A: Because those spiders are very shy. I stood looking at it for some time. It made me nervous but fascinated. Then I realised there were many spiders all hanging upside down under the beams!

B: Oh.

A: I thought the only explanation can be they've got too hot. The spiders have got too hot and they've come out of their holes, and climbed underneath, to escape the heat. I could recognise their anxiety, at being so exposed.

From nowhere, B *hands a teacup to* A.

B: I hope that's how you like it. Sorry, no biscuits! I meant to buy some.

A: Perfect. You put the milk in first, I can tell.

B: Yes. Wow, you must drink a lot of tea.

A: Mmmn. I love tea. In fact, as I get older I seem to be drinking more and more. It's a perverse irony of nature that my consumption seems to be inversely proportional to the slackening of my pelvic floor.

B: [*knowingly*] Yes.

A: Tea is delicious. Such a simple pleasure. Yet it's no minor beverage.

B: I don't drink it much; [*She now has a coffee mug*] love a coffee though.

A: 'When tea becomes ritual, it takes its place at the heart of our ability to see greatness in small things.'

B: Really?

A: 'Where is beauty to be found? In great things that, like everything else, are doomed to die, or in small things that aspire to nothing, yet know how to set a jewel of infinity in a single moment?'

B: Very profound!

A: Muriel Barbery: *The Elegance of the Hedgehog*. The fact remains I love tea, even on a hot day.

B: Heat and hot drinks! I can't think of anything worse.

A: Don't you like the heat?

B: Yes I do, it makes me feel like I'm on holiday.

A: Really?

B: [*fondly*] Yes, as if my partner was still alive.

A: Oh…

    Pause.

B: It's okay.

A: Oh… is that what the card was for?

    Pause.

B: When I'm planning a trip, it's always to somewhere hot. Closer to the sun.

A: Really?

B: Once I went to an active volcano with a lake inside it. And inside the lake an island, and on the island a lake with an island in it. So I went there, and on the way—

A: To an active volcano?

B: Yeah, you can cook your breakfast on the rocks at the top.

A: Are you mad?

B: Possibly.

So I went there and it was humid; very sticky on the bus with all the people crammed in, so I got off early at a roadside stall to get some water and a shiny car pulled up, which was odd.

A: Why?

B: I hadn't seen a car since we left the city. And two men in suits got out, which was very odd way up in the mountains. And they spoke to the stallholder in a language I didn't understand, and one of them leaned forward and his jacket flapped open, and there was a gun in his inside pocket.

A: Maybe he was pleased to see you?

B: What?

A: Don't worry.

B: A real gun! What business were they up to?

A: Not your business.

B: Exactly… I wasn't there for a gunfight. So I stood back and let them get down the road before I headed off.

A: Good thinking.

B: I walked along the road with my water, thinking that no-one in the world, except the stallholder and the gunmen knew where I was.

A: How terrifying.

B: What?

A: Awful.

B: It was fine. And then suddenly I became aware of these spiders.

A: Spiders!

B: Thousands of them, strung across the road between the telegraph poles. Big and black, with long legs spread out, as if they were guarding the road. Or me. Or maybe they were ready to pounce.

A: No, they were guarding you. Or warning you not to go to the volcano.

B: I don't know, but when I finally got there everyone had gone and they'd put up a sign: Volcano closed.

A: Maybe that was for the best.

B: But I could see the steam. You can't close a volcano. Humans are funny.

Pause.

A: Yes. Yes, they are.

Some people I know bought an old house that hadn't been lived in for a while. There were a lot of spiders on the outside. Beautiful big golden orb spiders and others. They got the pest man over to spray a five metre radius around the house before they moved in. All gone.

B: All gone.

A: We really are… doomed.

They look into their cups.

Leaves fall.

Hyperspace:

A: I can hear you—life.

B: Life outside my door.

A: In the trees, under the floor.

B: Scuttling, singing, nestling.

A: Getting under my skin.

B: I know you are here.

A: Funny where you end up.

A pulse begins.

They sing and dance together, 'Not Dead Yet':

BOTH: I'm not dead yet

I'll tell you why

I'm not dead yet

I still cry

I'm not dead yet

I still wee-ee-eep

And I'm sure not dead when I can't get to sleep

I'm not dead yet

I'm facing facts

With footprints this deep

I can't cover my tracks

But I'm not dead yet

Know how I tell?

Come a little closer; cop this smell!

When I've had my day in the sun

When I'm ready to hand in my gun

When the silence finally comes

I'll give in

I'll give in

I'll give... in

But

I'm not dead yet

I'm wide awake

Can't even close my eyes for heaven's sake

I'm not dead yet

But just like you

If I look far enough ahead there's only one view

When I've had my day in the sun
When I'm ready to hand in my gun
When the silence finally comes
I'll give in
I'll give in
I'll give... in
But

I'm not dead yet
I'm wide awake
Can't even close my eyes for heaven's sake
I'm not dead yet
But just like you
If I look far enough ahead there's only one view
If I look far enough ahead there's only one view
If I look far enough ahead there's only one view-ew-ew

B *arrives at* A*'s place. She knocks.*

B: Hello?
   Hello-o!
   [*She knocks again.*] Are you there?
   Are you there?
A: [*from her chair*] Yes.
       B *enters.*

B: I had a dream about my surgeon.
A: Was it rude?
B: No. He has a rare night off. He creeps into his garage, not wanting anyone to see him.

A: That is a bit creepy.

B: There's a wall of precision instruments: shining scalpels, scissors, tweezers, clamps, needles and thread... and other fasteners: zips, hooks and eyes... Beneath them a pile of spare parts waiting to be selected and used...

A: Very creepy.

B: Pulsating hearts, lungs expanding and contracting, twitching toes, mouths forming words, pink, alive and ready to go... And a rack of clothes... and then I see that they're not clothes but... people, made from the bits and pieces in the garage. Repaired. Restored. Imperfect. Glorious.

> A *stares at* B.

What do you think? Say something.

A: I'm not sure what to say... It's macabre but beautifully complete, so full of potential.

B: Yes that's what I thought.

A: Every once in a while a dream can be that potent.

So—zips and fasteners but no buttons.

B: No.

A: Funny.

> *Pause.*

I had a dream many years ago about my mum. She died.

B: In the dream?

A: No. She really died.

B: Oh I'm sorry.

A: Yes it was awful. We lived together; I nursed her to death.

B: What!

A: I mean to the end. Ghastly... protracted. Anyway I was very upset when she was finally taken and then I had this dream.

B: What was it?

A: There were five glass phone boxes in a row. I was just standing near them for some reason when number two phone-box rang. I thought I'd better answer it. There was no-one else around. I stepped inside and I saw my mum on the phone in number five. She looked different. I said into the mouthpiece 'Hello Mum, you look very tired and wrinkled.' She said, 'That's because I've been amongst the ashes'.

B: Oh.

A: I felt really silly because it was so obvious, she'd been cremated.

Then I thought—ah, I know now, she really has gone.

B: It must have been hard for you without your mum.

A: Just life taking its course. It must be hard for you without your partner.

B: Well it wasn't a firestorm, a flood, an earthquake. Not a war, a massacre, a planned attack. Not deceit, betrayal, abandonment… just life taking its course.

An awkward silence.

Then A *searches urgently.*

What are you doing?

A: I can't find it.

B: Find what?

A: I can't find the bloody heart. I can't make them without it.

B: Make what?

A: Shortbread hearts with cachous, shortbread hearts with cachous! I can't find the tin heart-shaped bloody biscuit cutter! I can't make them without it. It won't be the same. It's different, wrong. All the effort, energy, love that's gone into this and the heart is missing.

B: Are you crying?

A: It's too late to do something else.

B: You could do Anzacs, they're easy.

A: It's not about easy. It's about care, detail, beauty, love. Anzacs are lumpy, ugly, pedestrian.

B: Are you okay?

A: I'm mad!

B: What, mad insane, or angry?

A: I'm all of it. Insane and angry!

She searches more frantically.

It's got to be here somewhere. It must be here somewhere. In a corner, a crack, a crease, the heart, the heart, the heart.

B: Can I get you some tea?

A: What?!

B: Greatness in small things. 'Where is beauty to be found?'

A: Not here, that's for sure!

B: Your quote about tea.

A: It doesn't matter. It's gone. I've lost it. I'm too intense. Too weird. I say the wrong things. I expose too much.

B: What do you mean?

A: The heart. My heart. I undid my buttons and let them see in.

B: Who?

A: They laughed when they saw what was underneath.

B: I'm sorry.

A: And now it's too late.

B: It's not too late. The world goes on!

A holds B's gaze: a faceoff.

A: Yes. Doesn't it?

B: Yes. It's never too late.

A: Piffle!

B: No—listen to me.

A: Why should I?

B: I was walking… eucalyptus, foliage, feathers, magpie talk and then… human moaning—a couple doing it in the bushes. Their glasses click against each other. They're in their mid-seventies, easily: slack skin, stiff joints, crooked arthritic fingers, but the tenderness…

A: I can hear you thinking.

B: I'm speaking. Smells of armpits and lavender. Hands squeezing tissue thin skin. Gripping and gasping. In the leaf litter, amongst the humus and bird bones.

A: Shoosh!

B: In the dirt.

A: I don't want to know.

B: I want that. Before the worms get me. Before I turn to dust.

A: Shutup!

B: I'm talking to you.

A: Shut your mouth, shut ya face, shut ya gob, cake-hole, pie-hole.

Shut your bone-box, shut the hell up, shut yer cock-holster!

Shut your mouth before the birds nest in it. Shut the fuck up!

Stop ya gawping!

Hold your tongue, you're speaking shit, verbal diarrhoea, diatribe, mouth like a sewer. What a load of codswallop.

Have you got your period, is it that time, are you pre-menstrual, menopausal?

Is it a full moon… AHOOH!

Calm down, listen to yourself.

Button it!

B: Shutup!

A: Button it!

B: Go away!

A: Button it!

> B *blocks her ears.*

Button! Button!

She waves her shirt buttons at B.

B: GO AWAY!!

She pushes A *into her chair.*

A *disappears into the chair.*

B *peers after her;* MUSICIAN *peers also.*

Are you there?

Are you there?

I'm sorry.

B gingerly sits in A*'s chair.*

The musician sings, 'Am I Here':

MUSICIAN: Am I here?

Am I here?

Am I anywhere?

I'm not all there

But I'm not a chair

Am I done

Or undone?

Am I in the clear?

Can I take a guess?

Should I be depressed?

Time and space

Space and time

Nothing there at all

What's a life?

Just a little time

And if no-one cares

Then am I here?

Am I on?

Am I off?

Do I have a choice?

Can I take a test?

Can I take a rest?

Am I old?

Am I sold?

Have I drained away?

I can't remember yesterday

MUSICAN *and* B: [*together*] Time and space

Space and time

B: Nothing comes to mind

Am I loved?

Am I left behind?

And if no-one cares

Will I disappear?

Am I here?

Am I here?

Am I anywhere?

If no-one cares

Then I'm not here

B *confesses to the audience.*

B: I have a phobia. I don't know why. It's more common than you'd think. I don't talk about it. People think it's only a... button. Not a spider or snake, not the unspeakable, the end of the world. Most people don't understand. My partner did. My partner understood.

When I was young, if I touched one I'd shudder violently. I'd have to wash my hands, get it off. If my mother was wearing a cardigan I'd scream when she picked me up. I couldn't go near my dad when he put on a work shirt. It was okay when they were covered by his tie, but if one was peering out I'd cringe and run away.

I rub my fingers together and I'm okay. The clear plastic ones with four holes are the worst; I don't know why. They make my skin crawl, like touching a cockroach. When I see them I need to absorb a non-b... area to get rid of the insult in my eyes—the sea, the sky, the Great Big Nothing.

I don't even like it in other languages—'Knopf' in German.

Saying the word makes my throat tighten.

B... button...

A *'s button appears at* B *'s feet.*

Hello? Are you there?

Are you there?

She eyes the button.

My heart is jumping, I might be sick. I can't.

I'm sorry. I can't bear them, even the smell.

People say it's just a little disc. It can't hurt you—it's a thing. A beautiful thing, a useful thing... it keeps things together.

Not me. Makes me fall apart. Makes me the odd one out, mad. Am I mad?

A *reappears.*

A tender gestural sequence during which A *magically 'sews' her button onto* B's *polar fleece.*

A: Don't be afraid; people have been doing this forever. All you need is a needle and some thread and then follow the steps. You'll see there's nothing to it.

Choose a button if you don't have the original.

Cut a piece of thread about half a yard long.

Feed the thread through the eye of the needle.

Slide the needle to the middle.

Tie a knot where both ends meet.

Tie another knot, so that the end is doubly secure.

The thread is now ready to sew.

Place the button on top of the material where you intend to sew it. A match in between the button and the material will give it the necessary slack.

From underneath, push the needle up and into one of the holes.

Pull until the knot is anchored.

Push the needle down through the next hole.

End with the needle on the material side.

Secure with a double knot.

B: If I could just touch it. I know what I can see is not all there is.

A: Energy surging back and forth.

B: Buzzing. Glowing. Spinning.

A: Electrons, neutrons, protons.

B: Daring me.

A: Driving me.

BOTH: I've been here so long.

B: How long has it been?

A: The world has changed but the button is here, waiting.

B: Perhaps a joke could lighten the situation.

A: It's a long time since I told one of those… only one comes to mind…

B: Go on, tell it.

A: Well, a mushroom goes to a nightclub and the bouncer says at the door 'You can't come in. We don't want your sort here.' And the mushroom says 'But why? I'm a fun guy!'

They sing together, acknowledging each other, moving separately but in unison: 'In Between'.

BOTH: This is not how it begins

This is not the final scene

It's just a song to sing

In between

Did I just hear what you said?

Should I intervene?

Is it all in my head?

Do I live in between?

Splitting headache, splitting hairs

Splitting atoms, say your prayers

Is anyone there?

Hundreds of birds in the trees

Galaxies we can't see

All the people we could be

We live in between

I'm watching the sky

I'm watching planets die

Look up

Say goodbye

Time gets in through the cracks

Making maps on our skin

Right now the sun warms my back

We live in between

We live in between

We live…

They are sitting in each other's chairs.

B: I know you're there.

A: How are you?

B: Holding together. You?

A: Insane. Angry.

B: Yes.

A: Here we are.

B: We're still here.

A: Bodies with heads.

B: Bodies with heads.

A: Funny where you end up.

B: Is this the end?

THE END

⊕ LA MAMA

presents

Button

29 May–16 June 2013

Devisor / Performers
Carole Patullo, Jane Bayly

Dramaturg / Director
Melanie Beddie

Musician / Sound Designer
Peter Farnan

Lighting Designer
Katie Sfetkidis

Choreographer
Luke George

Designer
Melanie Liertz

With

Chairs **Daniele Poidomani**
Magic Consultant **Alex de la Rambelje**
Photographer **Deryk McAlpin, Proof**
Image Design **Robin Griffiths at DazzleCreative.com.au**

LA MAMA

Level 1, 205 Faraday Street, Carlton VIC 3053
www.lamama.com.au info@lamama.com.au
facebook.com/lamama.theatre twitter.com/lamamatheatre
Office phone 03 9347 6948 Office Hours Mon–Fri, 10:30am–5:30pm

CEO & Artistic Director
Liz Jones

Company Manager & Creative Producer
Pippa Bainbridge

Administration Coordinator
Laura Smith

Communications Coordinator
Nedd Jones

House Managers
Lisa Höbartner & Rebecca Etchell

La Mama Learning Producer
Maureen Hartley

Marketing Coordinator
Mary Helen Sassman

La Mama Community & Mobile Producer
Caitlin Dullard

Preservation Coordinator
Fiona Wiseman

La Mama for Kids Curator
Ella Holmes

La Mama Musica Producer
Annabel Warmington

La Mama Poetica Curator
Matt Hetherington

Script Appraiser
Graham Downey

FRONT OF HOUSE STAFF:

The regular staff and Jo-Anne Armstrong, Phoenix Bade, Susan Bamford-Caleo, Alex Desebrock, Carmelina Di Guglielmo, Nicola Gunn, Tanya Harrowell, Amber Hart, Laura Hegyesi, Mari Lourey, Phil Roberts, Laurence Strangio, Raymond Triggs, Annabel Warmington and Canada White.

COMMITTEE OF MANAGEMENT:

Sue Broadway, Dur-é Dara, Mark Rubbo, Caroline Lee, Kerry Noonan, Adam Cass, Rhonda Day and Liz Jones.

La Mama's Committee of Management, staff and its wider theatrical community acknowledge that our theatre is on traditional Wurundjeri land.

La Mama is financially assisted by the Australian Government through the Australia Council—its arts funding and advisory body, the Victorian Government through Arts Victoria—Department of Premier and Cabinet, and the City of Melbourne through the Arts and Culture triennial funding program.

Australian Government

Australia Council for the Arts

ARTS VICTORIA

Victoria The Place To Be

CITY OF MELBOURNE

CAROLE PATULLO
DEVISOR / PERFORMER

JANE BAYLY
DEVISOR / PERFORMER

Carole is an actor, improviser, writer and teacher. She first performed at La Mama in 1985 in *Making the Jump* by Ian Nash. Recent La Mama performances include *Charitable Intent* by David Williamson and *Shedding* by Melissa Bubnic, both of which earned Carole Green Room Award nominations. Other theatre includes *Storming St Kilda By Tram* (Theatreworks), *Geography* (Whistling in the Theatre), *After Dinner* and *Away* (MTC), *Chicago Chicago* (NYID), *In Cahoots*, *Blabbermouth*, *Electro Diva*, *Game Girl* (Arena TC), *A Black Joy* by Declan Greene, *A Man For All Seasons* (CWTC), *The Lost Story of the Magdalene Asylum* (Peepshow Inc.). Film and television appearances include *Lake Mungo*, *My Year Without Sex*, *Offspring*, *City Homicide*, *The Librarians* and *Winners and Losers*. Carole co-founded and was a core member of corporate improvisation company Troupe du Jour for 15 years, and she teaches regularly.

Jane is an actor, devisor, singer, songwriter and teacher. As a founding member of a cappella theatre company Crying in Public Places, she co-devised several shows and toured extensively. Recent La Mama performances include *Care Instructions* (with Aphids/Malthouse, Transit VI Festival, Denmark), *Miss Hewett's Shenanigans*, *The Chapel Perilous* (with Perilous Productions). This year Jane is touring with Donna Jackson's *Dust* (Hubcap Productions/ Right Angle Events). Other theatre includes *homeland*, *neither lost nor found* (Keene/Taylor Theatre Project), *Blabbermouth* (Arena Theatre/MTC), *Burn!* (HotHouse), *The Newspaper of Claremont St*, *King Lear* (Playbox), *The Women There*, *Brecht x2* (Arena Theatre), *Infectiou$* (Crying Out Loud), *Viva La Vida: Frida Kahlo* (Handspan), *STOMP!* (Yes/No People) and *The Sapphires* creative development (MTC). Recent screen credits include *The Time of Our Lives*, *The Wedding Party* and *The Slap*. Jane teaches for theatre companies, schools, community and corporate organisations. She was Director of the Monash Schools' Theatre Festival from 2008–12.

MELANIE BEDDIE
DRAMATURG / DIRECTOR

Melanie is a graduate of Sydney University and VCA. She was a co-founder of the $5 Theatre Co. and is Artistic Director of The Branch theatre company. She works as an actor, dramaturg and director. At La Mama she has directed *Geese and the Psych Ward* by Maxwell Silver, *Traitors by Stephen Sewell* (The Branch co-production, winner GreenRoom Best Director), *Sinners* by Ramez Tabit and Johann McIntyre and *Aviary*. Other work includes Ibsen's *Ghosts* (The Branch) *Second Childhood* by Morris Gleitzman (MTC/Hothouse), *The Raindancers* by Karen Mainwaring (MTC)*, Diving for Pearls* by Katherine Thompson (MTC), Pam Leversha's *Violet Inc.* (Playbox) and *Sisters of Gelam* by the Maza Sisters (Ilbijerri Theatre.) In 2002, with Paul Monaghan and Peter Eckersall, Melanie co-founded the Dramaturgies Forum, to examine Australian dramaturgical practice. Melanie received the Dramaturgy Fellowship from the Australia Council (2004) and a Gloria Fellowship from NIDA (2009). She was an inaugural board member of Playwriting Australia, is a long serving committee member of the Melbourne-based Green Room Awards and is a founding member of AWDA.

PETER FARNAN
MUSICIAN / SOUND DESIGNER

Peter is a theatre composer, musical director, sound designer, performer, producer and teacher. He has created scores and sound designs for La Mama (*Asylum, The Bridge*), Malthouse (*Woyzeck, Tartuffe, Sleeping Beauty*), MTC (*The Sapphires, Rockabye, Moonlight and Magnolias, All My Sons, The Clean House, Take Me Out, Boy Gets Girl, Hitchcock Blonde, Three Days Of Rain*), QTC (*Let the Sunshine*), Black Swan/Belvoir Company B (*The Sapphires*), *Back to Back/Theatre of Speed (DMI)*, National Institute of Circus Arts/Melbourne Festival (*Divino Cabaret*), OzOpera (*Way Deal Cool*) and Melbourne Fringe (*Infectiou$*). His work has been nominated for Helpmann and Green Room Awards. He is best known as guitarist and songwriter for rock band Boom Crash Opera. For Queensland Music Festival's Song Trails program, he designed and delivered songwriting workshops, recordings and concerts to regional and urban communities. He continues to perform his songs at large festivals and tiny gatherings. He currently teaches songwriting at NMIT and is completing a research Masters in Sound Design (Songwriting) at VCAM.

LUKE GEORGE
CHOREOGRAPHER

MELANIE LIERTZ
DESIGNER

Luke is a Melbourne-based dance artist. A graduate of the VCA, his practice as performer, choreographer, collaborator, teacher and curator has taken him throughout Australia, Europe, Asia and North America. As a choreographer George's work has been presented by Arts House, Dancehouse, PICA, Dance Massive, Next Wave Festival, Melbourne Fringe, 10 Days on the Island and he has performed short pieces in New York and Tokyo. Choreographic highlights include *Now Now Now* (2011), *Lifesize* (2007–09) and *Home* all of which have received Australian Dance and Green Room Award nominations. George has received several commissions including work with the Sydney Opera House and Lucy Guerin Inc. George has worked with acclaimed theatre companies such as Malthouse, Arena and Back to Back.

Melanie is a theatre and film designer (B Creative Arts, VCA 2001), who also creates custom fashion and wearable art. Set and costume designs include *She's Not Performing*, *Split*, *Darwin's Dangerous Idea* (La Mama), *Emporium of Treasures* (Rawcus), *One Day and The Dream Factory* (St Martins Youth Arts Centre), *One Cloud* (Theatreworks) and *On Intoxicated Ears* (45 Downstairs). Melanie has designed costumes for A is for Atlas (*Cherry Cherry*), Westside Circus (*Shadows on the Footpath*, *Escape Hatch*, *Tales from a Watertight World*) and designed many productions at Ballarat Arts Academy since 2008. She has also created costumes for the Australian Ballet, NICA and Victorian Opera.

KATIE SFETKIDIS
LIGHTING DESIGNER

Katie is a lighting designer and Live Artist, who has been working in the field of live art and experimental performance since graduating from Victorian College of the Arts in 2007. Career highlights include; *this is for you* (La Mama), *Tame* (Malthouse Theatre), *Happy Ending* (Melbourne Theatre Company), *The Laramie Project: 10 Years Later* (Red Stitch/ The Arts Centre), *Psycho Beach Party* (Little Ones Theatre), *These are the Isolate* (Mutation Theatre), *Elektra* (Fraught Outfit) and *Little Mercy* (Sisters Grimm). She has been nominated for three Green Room Awards and is a recipient of a number of awards and initiatives including: The Rory Dempster Lighting Internship, Malthouse Besen Family Artist Program, Australia Council Artstart and JUMP national mentoring program.

STANDING OVATION FOR
AUSTRALIA'S HOME OF INDEPENDENT THEATRE

In 2013, La Mama will celebrate 46 years of nurturing new Australian Theatre.

Built in 1883 for Anthony Reuben Ford, a Carlton printer, the building at 205 Faraday Street had been used as a workshop, a boot and shoe factory, an electrical engineering workshop and a silk underwear factory before becoming a theatre in 1967. La Mama was established by Betty Burstall and modelled on experimental theatre activities at La MaMa E.T.C., New York. Jack Hibberd's play *Three Old Friends* was the first play performed in the tiny space.

Since that time the crowded intimacy of La Mama has provided welcome opportunities to a host of playwrights, actors, directors, technicians, film-makers, poets and comedians, such as David Williamson, Barry Dickins, John Romeril, Tes Lyssiotis, Lloyd Jones, Arthur and Corinne Cantrill, Judith Lucy, Richard Frankland, Julia Zemiro, and Cate Blanchett... the list of those who have been nurtured there is long.

Under the capable care of Liz Jones (Artistic Director since 1976), and her La Mama team, more than 50 productions are now produced annually at La Mama, and at our second performance venue, the refurbished La Mama Courthouse, 349 Drummond Street. An ever-increasing audience is drawn not only from the Carlton and Melbourne University environs, but from far and wide across the country.

'I set La Mama up, as a space for writers and directors to perform in but also it was a space where people came, as audience, to participate in the creative experiment.'

—Betty Burstall, 1987, Artistic Director of La Mama
1967–76

'Much will be said of La Mama's role in developing a new generation of Australian writing. However, in considering policies and personalities, one should not forget the nature of the space and its impact in making possible performances that would be lost in a large theatre. It gave performances the intimacy of the cinema close-up with the exciting immediacy of the live theatre and the warmth of the coffee lounge.'

—Daryl Wilkinson, 1986, Director
From *La Mama... The story of a Theatre*

La Mama Theatre—which, on various occasions, has been called headquarters, the source, the shopfront and the birthplace of Australian theatre—was classified by the National Trust in 1999.

'The two story brick building is of State cultural significance because it has been occupied by La Mama Theatre... The building is indelibly associated with the performance arts and is a rare manifestation of an experimental theatre in Australia...'

—National Trust Classification Report

When it comes to grassroots Melbourne theatre, La Mama in Carlton is like the 60GB iPod – small, subtle, but containing a whole lot more than you might expect.

—John Bailey, The *Age*. E.G. 29/06/05

La Mama produces work from two venues: 205 Faraday Street, Carlton (opposite top), and at the La Mama Courthouse, 349 Drummond Street, Carlton.

For current La Mama productions and events, see www.lamama.com.au.

From Frankston Arts Centre season, Cube 37, 2012: Not Dead Yet:
Peter Farnan, Carole Patullo and Jane Bayly (Cube 37, Frankston Arts Centre,
2012). Photo by Deryk McAlpin

From La Mama Explorations season 2011 Wide shot 8411:
Carole Patullo, Jane Bayly and Peter Farnan (La Mama Explorations season,
2011). Photo by Dayna Morrissey

CP standing, JB behind chair 8444: Carole Patullo and Jane Bayly (La Mama Explorations season, 2011). Photo by Dayna Morrissey

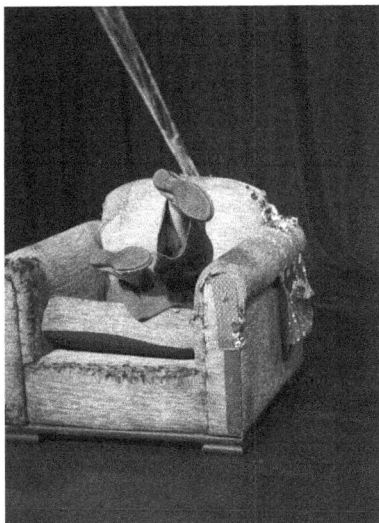

Feet: Carole Patullo (Cube 37, Frankston Arts Centre, 2012). Photo by Deryk McAlpin

Guns: Carole Patullo and Jane Bayly (Cube 37, Frankston Arts Centre, 2012). Photo by Deryk McAlpin

OTHER TITLES IN THE 2013 CURRENT THEATRE SERIES AVAILABLE FROM CURRENCY PRESS

FORGET ME NOT BY TOM HOLLOWAY

I came home from work and you were gone.

Gerry is around 60. He left Liverpool, UK, when he was three. Mary is in her 80s and has never stopped celebrating her little boy's birthday, despite the fact that she came home from work one day and he was gone.

Tom Holloway's exquisit play draws on the true stories of the 3,000+ British children who, between the end of the Second World War and 1970, were told they were orphans and were shipped to Australia on a promise of warmth, fresh air, abundant food and boundless opportunity. Instead, lives of neglect and abuse awaited them.

A series of raw, achingly beautiful conversations between members of a scattered family, *Forget Me Not* is one man's precarious bid to learn what it means to love.

THE BULL, THE MOON AND THE CORONET OF STARS BY VAN BADHAM

Alone in the museum, in the dark, Marion unravels a ball of string so Michael can venture into a mystery. In recent weeks, strange stirrings have haunted the ancient relics and rumours of a monster abound. Michael finds his way back to her and into an impossible situation.

Marion flees and finds herself the prim centre of an over-sexed septuagenarian art group at a seaside resort. Here, Marion is infuriated by Mark, a wayward sommelier with an eye for the ladies, determined to disrupt her lessons and her life.

Whimsical, sensual and charmingly humourous, *The Bull, the Moon and the Coronet of Stars* is a love story of mythic proportions. It will lure you into an orgy of antiquity, cupcakes and beach side frivolity.

DREAMS IN WHITE BY DUNCAN GRAHAM

When wealthy property developer Michael Devine goes missing, his wife Anne and daughter Amy fear the worst.

As the pieces of Michael's disappearance start falling into place, the picture reveals a scandalous secret.

On the other side of town, Paula and Gary Anderson have an unwanted visitor. Regretting ever having let Ray Wimple creep into their lives, they're now stuck with his unwelcome and insistent attention.

When these two very different worlds collide, one fateful event will transform both families forever.

Inspired by true events *Dreams in White* is a griping thriller of double lives and urban alienation.

www.ingramcontent.com/pod-product-compliance
Lightning Source LLC
Chambersburg PA
CBHW041934090426
42744CB00017B/2061